LOVELY LAMBETH

South London Walks

Jon Newman

Thamesis
WALKIES

Thamesis

First published 2017
by Thamesis Publications
3b Webber Street
London SE1 8PZ
www.thamesispublications.co.uk

ISBN 978-0-9927045-3-7

Printed by Imprint Digital
www.imprintdigital.net
Design by Silbercow www.silbercow.co.uk

Supported using public funding by
**ARTS COUNCIL
ENGLAND**

THAMESIS WALKIES

Battersea Nocturne by Jon Newman (978-0-9927045-4-4)
Lost in Herne Hill by Jon Newman (978-0-9927045-5-1)

LOVELY LAMBETH

The poet and artist, William Blake, was born in Westminster in 1757. He was apprenticed as an engraver and earned his living designing book illustrations for London publishers. However he also became a self-published poet and artist, using novel etching and printing techniques to write, illustrate and produce his own work. He moved to Lambeth in February 1791 to live with his wife in Hercules Buildings (now Hercules Road). His modest terraced house doubled as home and studio and from it, in arguably what would be his most productive decade, he created many of his most famous monotypes known as the 'Large Colour Prints', such as *Newton* and *Nebuchadnezzar*, now in Tate Britain. Here too he refined his system of relief etching to produce *Songs of Innocence and of Experience*, *Europe*, *America* and many other of his self-published 'prophetic books'. He left Lambeth in 1800 to spend three years living and working in Sussex, before returning to Westminster where he died in 1827.

Much of Blake's most accessible poetry can be found in *Songs of Innocence and of Experience*, which he self-published from Hercules Buildings in 1794. In that work the later Experience poems, written while he was living in Lambeth offer a more bitter worldly counterpoint to the naive pastoral of the *Songs of Innocence*, conceived six years earlier when he was in Westminster. Brought together in a single volume they represented for Blake, "the two contrary states of the human soul", with deliberate echoes and antitheses between the two halves: *Infant Joy* becoming *Infant Sorrow*; *The Lamb* mutating into *The Tyger*.

The short lyric *London* from *The Songs of Experience* is now recognised as one of the earliest expressions of the condition that we have come to call 'urban'. In it a host of familiars – the poor, the disenfranchised, the damaged, the sick at heart and the exploited – are encountered wandering the streets of the city.

LONDON

I wander thro' each charter'd street,
Near where the charter'd Thames does flow.
And mark in every face I meet
Marks of weakness, marks of woe.

In every cry of every Man,
In every Infants cry of fear,
In every voice: in every ban,
The mind-forg'd manacles I hear

How the Chimney-sweepers cry
Every blackning Church appalls,
And the hapless Soldiers sigh
Runs in blood down Palace walls

But most thro' midnight streets I hear
How the youthful Harlots curse
Blasts the new-born Infants tear
And blights with plagues the Marriage hearse

Where all the other 'songs' in *Innocence and Experience* have
been given titles that are abstracts or archetypes, *London* is the
only poem about a specific place. So it is odd that while
referencing the city and its river, what Blake actually describes is
an eerily anonymous space through which a bewildered wanderer
passes. The other paradox, and one that will be explored on this
walk, is that the poem called 'London' was not only conceived and
written in Lambeth but was also, arguably, imaginatively located
within that place.

Life mask of William Blake made in 1823
when he was fifty six years old

Begin at the north east corner of Westminster Bridge beneath the South Bank Lion

"From Lambeth we began our foundations, Lovely Lambeth"

The foot of Westminster Bridge is an appropriate point to begin, beneath the South Bank Lion. This wandering Lambeth orphan, a Coadestone advertisement, was salvaged from the top of the bombed-out Lion brewery when it was cleared for the Festival of Britain in 1950 and then planted before Waterloo Station. It was set here with gilt letters and gravitas in 1966.

To stand by the river in Lambeth and to look across to Westminster is to engage with a very familiar image of London. Think of those opening film shots tracking a red bus past Big Ben or the talking head on the TV news before a backdrop of Parliament – they were all filmed from the Lambeth side. The young Turner painted a watercolour of the bridge and Westminster from this same view point in 1796 when he was just 21. Which makes it difficult to re-imagine how, when Blake crossed this bridge to move to Lambeth in the winter of 1790–1791, it was still an alarmingly new connection between London and a curious new suburb that was just starting to be built.

Westminster Bridge, one of only three London Thames crossings, connected Surrey with the cities of Westminster and London, linking and yet also keeping them separate. It was only six years older than Blake himself, and most of the new suburb of Lambeth that it led to post-dated its construction. We still carry a version of the divide between North and South London, but it is difficult to appreciate just how strangely new a place Blake was entering into when in 1790 he abandoned Westminster and crossed the river in a cart with his wife, a few household goods and his rolling press.

One of the reasons Blake moved to Lambeth was its affordability. The first flurry of grand ribbon development along the southern approach roads to the Bridge had given way to a second stage of development: modest terraces of houses behind the main roads, laid out on the newly-drained fields of what had been Lambeth

Marsh. The three-storey house that Blake moved into at Hercules Buildings was one such, perched on the edge of this new world that was still being built. It had views across fields to the front, a garden at the back and offered much more space and, crucially for the artist, light than he could afford back in Westminster.

Lambeth was not unknown to Blake. As a boy he had rambled out of London: north to the fields that would shortly be given over for Regents Park and south across the new bridge, through Lambeth to Dulwich and the hills of Norwood and Sydenham. It was memories of the fields at North London's rural edge that inspired his lyric in *Jerusalem*,

> *The fields from Islington to Marybone,*
> *To Primrose Hill and Saint Johns Wood:*
> *Were builded over with pillars of gold,*
> *And there Jerusalems pillars stood.*

He never wrote in a similar vein about South London, but it was on Peckham Rye Common, as he later recalled, that he had a childhood vision of "a tree filled with angels, bright angelic wings bespangling every bough like stars". On a different South London expedition he came upon the prophet Ezekiel seated beneath a tree and on another visionary occasion saw "the haymakers at work, and amid them angelic figures walking". Later and more prosaically as a young man aged 25 he would cross the bridge to Lambeth to walk out to Battersea to court and eventually marry Catherine Boucher.

The contrast between Lambeth and his home in Westminster was immense. When he had lived around Broad Street and Golden Square, Blake had been an engraver among fellow artists. William Hogarth and Sir Joshua Reynolds had both lived on Leicester Square, as would Blake's friend the sculptor John Flaxman; another friend, the artist Henry Fuseli lived on Broad Street (where Blake had been born) as would later John Varley; Paul Sandby lived on Poland Street (as would Blake briefly in the 1780s) and Angelica Kauffmann had a house on Golden Square. In leaving this network of streets, Blake was abandoning artist friends and professional acquaintances and uncoupling himself from booksellers like Joseph Johnson at St Paul's Church Yard, Miller at Old Bond Street and Edwards on New Bond Street who had been his main sources of jobbing employment as an engraver. For whatever reasons, he had abandoned this established artistic milieu and was now south of the river in a less fashionable region of newly-built streets occupied by small traders and shopkeepers.

Walk east along the side of Westminster Bridge Road, past the former County Hall building and then turn left into Belvedere Road; take the first right into Forum Magnum Square and cross over York Road at the other end of the square to the former Westminster Lying In Hospital

The construction of Westminster Bridge (1751) and then Blackfriars Bridge (1768) had helped create a development bonanza in Lambeth by opening up its cheaper building land. One of the unintended consequences of this had been the decision by many major metropolitan charities to set up in or relocate their institutions to newly accessible and affordable Lambeth.

The Westminster, latterly the General, Lying In Hospital (the building is now part of the hotel next door) is one of the few surviving buildings from this charitable migration into Lambeth. The other is the former Bedlam Asylum building which relocated from the City to Lambeth Road in 1812 and now houses the Imperial War Museum. The Lying In Hospital, "licensed for the public reception of pregnant women" had first opened in Lambeth in 1765 to provide midwifery for poor pregnant women; the present building was constructed in 1828. Unusually – and this troubled the rate-payers of Lambeth fearful of funding a flood of pauper single-mothers – the hospital also accepted unmarried pregnant women.

As such, it was indirectly linked with two other Lambeth charities that Blake would also have known. The Westminster Female

Orphan Asylum (1758) stood at the junction of Lambeth Road and Kennington Road just beyond Blake's back garden (where the spire of Christchurch now stands). The other was the Magdalen Home for Penitent Prostitutes (relocated here 1772) around the corner on Blackfriars Road, and which Blake would have passed when he walked to Joseph Johnson's bookshop for his engraving work.

Shared Lambeth location aside, what really connected these three institutions was the way each of them was a response to the different casualties of London street prostitution. The Lying In Hospital provided a secure space for women to give birth in; the Magdalen Home provided rehabilitation for women sex workers escaping the economy of the street. This required visible penitential submission as a uniformed 'charitable object' while being trained in needlework and laundry for future work as a servant. Sunday service at the Magdalen chapel – just like visiting days at Bedlam or hanging days at Kennington – was a voyeur's destination, ogling the penitents in the front pews in their distinctive grey dresses with white bonnets and tippets.

Where the other two charities dealt with the direct casualties of prostitution, the Female Asylum's role was preventative. Orphan girls in London were extremely vulnerable to ending up as prostitutes. In the language of the day, the asylum saw its role as preserving 'friendless and deserted girls from those dangers and misfortunes to which their condition exposes them'. As with the Magdalen, the only available respectable outcome was a life as a servant. Girls were admitted at the age of nine and at fifteen they were bound apprentice for seven years to a life of domestic service.

The significance of these institutions to Blake can be seen in some of the poems in *Songs of Experience*. *Holy Thursday* is a reworking of a poem of the same title in Innocence which Blake had previously illustrated with a garland of Charity children, the girls in their mob caps and tippets not unlike the uniform of the Female Orphan Asylum. By contrast, the *Holy Thursday* of *Experience* is a much angrier poem,

Is this a holy thing to see
In a rich and fruitful land
Babes reduc'd to misery,
Fed with a cold and usurous hand?'

In the final verse of *London,* Blake offers a commentary on the dehumanising effects of the sex industry where the 'youthful harlot' destroys the innocence of childhood as well as the loving relationship of marriage.

But most through midnight streets I hear
How the youthful Harlot's curse
Blasts the new born Infant's tear
And blights with plagues the marriage hearse

Did Blake's exposure to the casualties and victims of prostitution – the visible uniformed 'objects' of the charitable institutions on the streets that surrounded his house – inform this final verse of the poem? He was walking past the human evidences every day.

Inmates of the Westminster Female Orphan Asylum next to Hercules Buildings. From a drawing by Thomas Rowlandson, 1808

Walk north along York Road past the hotel and take the first right into Leake Street. Its underground passage passes beneath the platforms of Waterloo Station through a space which, since the 2008 "Cans Festival", has become an "authorised graffiti area" for street artists. Stay on the left hand side of the walkway, pass under the taxi ramp and emerge onto Lower Marsh

If he were to be imaginatively summoned back, Blake might just about recognise the ancient street line of Lower Marsh with its late-eighteenth and early-nineteenth century frontages. This was the road that led east towards St George's Fields. He might even make out the original pub name (minus the ungulate) in the signboard for the Camel and Artichoke. Perhaps he would be reminded of the "contrary states of the human soul" in the counterpoints of Lower Marsh's street life: a few market barrows maintaining the coster illusion, a closed public library, a pawn brokers and betting shops, a coffee roastery, purveyors of vintage trinkets and a knitting shop, all set among the faux-cobbles, gun posts and retro-lamp standards of a 'London Street Market'.

Turn right from Leake Street and walk south along Lower Marsh, cross Westminster Bridge Road and go into Carlisle Lane, which is the left-hand of the two small roads opposite. Pass back under the line of the railway, turn left into Centaur Street and pass once again beneath the railway to arrive at Hercules Road

In Blake's time the medieval relic of Carlisle House was still standing. Originally the Bishop of Rochester's London dwelling, it had declined from episcopal residence to pottery, to brothel, to dancing master's academy and was now functioning as a boys' boarding school by the 1790s. Centaur Street, by contrast, was still part of the open fields that Blake looked across to from his new home. Today, populating the dark walls of the Carlisle Lane and Centaur Street railway bridges are the artworks of 'Project Blake', created by South Bank Mosaics between 2006 and 2014. Here are interpretations in mosaic of illustrations taken from the books that Blake was working on at Hercules Buildings between 1791 and 1800. One can find versions of plates from *America, Europe, The Visions of the Daughters of Albion, The Book of Thel* and *The Songs of Innocence and of Experience*. More of these Blake mosaics can be found beneath the Virgil Street railway bridge which runs parallel with Centaur Street and which can be accessed from further down Carlisle Lane.

Turn left onto Hercules Road and cross over to where a blue plaque on Blake House, a block of red brick flats, marks the site of Blake's house at 13 Hercules Buildings

To walk down Hercules Road is to follow the field line of suburban opportunism. The hedgerow, seen in the foreground of Hollar's 1670 panorama becomes the brick-earth digging on Rocque's 1750 map. Westminster Bridge opened in that year and its access roads south of the river created an irresistible development urge. Hercules Buildings was one of the first fruits, laid out down one side of a triangular plot which had become amputated from a larger field by the line of Kennington Road, itself the new link road cutting south from Westminster Bridge to the old coach road at Kennington. For Blake too Lambeth was opportune. It was his way out of cramped Westminster to a life in a less fashionable area perhaps, but one in which he could afford to rent a entire terraced house, with a kitchen in the basement and two rooms on each of its three floors. Crucially, the ground-floor front room was large enough to accommodate his engraver's wooden rolling press.

Twenty year's earlier he had begun his apprenticeship as an engraver and was by now skilled at translating other artists' work through the medium of engraved copper plates into book illustrations or prints. Such work required little more than a table in a well-lit room, the printing was done elsewhere. But Blake was not just a jobbing engraver doing piece-work for others – he was an artist and a poet in his own right. He might labour over other men's work in the day, but he would work through the night on his own work. After his youthful *Poetical Sketches* were published in 1783, he had realised that his poetic and artistic vision was unlikely to attract patronage or commercial publishing. Instead he was developing a means of self-publishing that could let him write, draw and print his own work on his own terms and combined into a single form.

His first experiments in what he would describe as 'Illuminated Printing', had been made in 1788–9 while in Westminster: *The Songs of Innocence* and *The Book of Thel*, both published by Blake in 1789, were two small exquisitely printed and hand-coloured booklets which combined etched text and illustration within the same plate. Blake's new technique of relief etching used an acid-resistant varnish to draw the design and write the (mirrored) text onto a copper plate; the remaining surface of the plate was then etched in acid so that the lines and text stood out in raised relief (the obverse of the conventional intaglio method of etching). Blake developed this into an affordable means of producing his books with all the processes carried out by himself. The copper plates he etched for the *Songs of Innocence and of Experience* were a mere 5" x 3", yet the press that he printed them on filled his whole room.

Blake's house on Hercules Road just prior to demolition, ca 1915

The title page of the combined edition of *Songs of Innocence and of Experience* that Blake produced in Lambeth in 1794 bears the colophon *The Author & Printer W Blake*. In an age of desktop- and self-publishing we have lost the sense of oddness that this statement must have had, suggesting as it did that an author had taken control of the means of production.

Subsequently, the small volumes that would emerge from the front room of Hercules Buildings (*America a Prophecy, Europe a Prophecy, The First Book of Urizen, The Visions of the Daughters of Albion, The Song of Los* and *The Book of Ahania*) would all carry on their title page the words LAMBETH Printed by William Blake, in the year... There is something that is both strange and almost defiant in this acknowledging of Lambeth as their place of creation. Publishers printed and published books in London or Edinburgh, in Amsterdam or Paris. No one produced or acknowledged literature in an unremarkable South London suburb like Lambeth – except Blake.

A plate from America, a Prophecy, one of the books that Blake wrote, designed and printed at Hercules Buildings, 1794

Walk north along Hercules Road back towards Westminster Bridge Road. Turn right through the metal gate between the end of Blake House and no. 1 Hercules Road. Turn right again and follow the line of raised flower beds at the back of the flats to a grass mound surrounded by a group of plane trees

We are standing on the site of Blake's back garden. Each of the houses of Hercules Buildings had a long thin strip of garden ground; Blake's house was just to the right of the covered gated passage that divides the middle of the block of flats. This was the first house he had lived in with a garden; there was a small summer house at the bottom and the fig tree and the vine growing there were a particular delight.

Hercules Buildings by its nature had mostly attracted middling folk, small builders, shop keepers and tradesmen, but set among them was the occasional wealthier entrepreneur. Such was Philip Astley, a cashiered cavalryman who on returning from the Seven Years War in 1763 started making a living from his horse riding skills that eventually became *Astley's Amphitheatre*, the world's first fixed site circus on Westminster Bridge Road at the corner of Stangate. From this success he had built himself a mansion in the triangle of land behind Hercules Buildings in the1780s. His house stood where the children's play area now is along the line of Cosser Street. "Hercules Hall", like Hercules Buildings, may have taken its name from the Hercules pub that stood on the corner but may also celebrate one of the acrobatic turns performed at Astley's: The Pillars of Hercules, where a group of athletes balance on one another's shoulders.

Astley's house was imposing enough in a new-moneyed way to have been recorded by several artists. However its entrance, via an alley squeezed between nos. 14 and 15 Hercules Buildings, was functional rather than grand and meant that Blake's back windows looked over Astley's premises. This proximity prompted one of the very few known incidents that give any sense of Blake interacting with his Lambeth neighbours. Once, looking up from his work table in the back room, Blake saw a servant boy in Astley's grounds hobbled with a log 'such as one puts on an ass or a horse'. He was furious at the injustice of this treatment, his 'blood boiled', and he went down the garden and raged at Astley's wife. That evening Philip came round to tell Blake to mind his own business; the stand-up row saw Astley concede the injustice of his treatment of the boy and Blake acknowledge his wrath – and peace was restored.

Continue to walk south west along the back of Blake House and exit through another gate onto Cosser Street. Turn right down Cosser Street to rejoin Hercules Road by the side of the Pineapple PH

The Pineapple pub is a late-nineteenth century rebuild of a beer-house that was here in Blake's time. Even though it is a later building, one can get a sense of the scale of the original street line of Hercules Buildings from the height and alignment of its lounge bar, just as at the other end of the terrace one can see it in the remains of no. 1 Hercules Road, once part of the former Hercules pub, now a sushi restaurant. The line of the alley that led between nos. 14 and 15 Hercules Buildings to Astley's house, Hercules Hall, also survives as a residual right of way as the covered passage running through the middle of Blake House.

Turn left onto Hercules Road and walk its length south to Lambeth Road

The large hotel development opposite Blake House has replaced a former government building, but its long, narrow triangular footprint is a reminder of its earlier pre-War use as the platforms of the Necropolis Railway Company, bombed beyond repair in 1941. This was a private cemetery and railway company that offered fashionably discreet interments by train: delivering cortege and mourners by private train from Waterloo to its cemetery at Brookwood in Surrey. The company's headquarters building still stands on Westminster Bridge Road. Blake, in hellish proverbial mood, advised to "Drive your cart and your plow over the bones of the dead". Future occupants of the "upper upscale" hotel rooms of the Park Plaza Waterloo will be suspended above the ghosts of their railway carriages instead.

The houses further down the opposite side of Hercules Buildings were built early in the nineteenth century after Blake had moved away and before the Southampton Railway shouldered its two mile viaduct through Vauxhall and Lambeth in 1847 to create its new terminus at Waterloo. By the time Blake's first biographer came to visit the area in the 1850s, its railway-tainted decline was only too apparent. For Gilchrist, the road was devoid of interest, "a row of houses sprung up since his [Blake's] boyish rambles... modest, irregular sized... since partly rebuilt, partly removed... now sordid and dirty [and] bestridden by the arches of the South Western Railway". Stepping gingerly across the river out of his metropolitan comfort-zone, he noted "the adjacent main roads, grimy and hopeless looking, stretch out their long arms towards further mile on mile of suburbs – Newington, Kennington, Brixton".

To walk on down the south side of Hercules Road is to pass through the changing versions of twentieth century public housing. The architecture of the Blake Estate built by the Corporation of London in the 1920s is in a "Homes-for-Heroes classical" style; south of Cosser Street the warm pink-red brick of the mansion blocks of the Briant Estate, with healthy gusts of breeze passing between their balconies and pram sheds, represents 1930's LCC "Slum clearance evangelical". Further south still on the other side of Lambeth Road is the "Post-war reconstruction" of the New China Walk estate: ranks of 1950s blocks diagonalised across what had been one of Lambeth's biggest and most famous bomb-sites. This hugely damaged area became the epitome of post-war London when, before the new flats were built, its extensively bombed dereliction served as the set for the 1949 film, 'Passport to Pimlico'. The badly damaged corner pub, visible throughout the film like a ruined landmark set in fields of broken brick, was the only survivor and, eventually patched up, is now the Corner Café.

Turn right onto and cross over Lambeth Road, walking west under the railway bridge

Squeezed between the pale post-war brickwork of New China Walk and the 1970s grey brutalism of no. 109 Lambeth Road, until recently the Metropolitan Police's forensic science service, is Pratt's Walk: a short stump of terrace that has survived from the late-eighteenth century. If Lambeth's or the LCC/GLC planners had got their way, it too would surely have been swept away in that self-assured bonfire of the productions of the late-18th and early-19th century speculative builders that would rage through South London. But rather curiously the houses of Pratt Walk escaped. With their three-storeyed flat fronts and basements, their simple door cases and triple windows, the houses are slightly grander and certainly better lit than those of Hercules Buildings. But in the absence of very much else remaining by way of local comparison, Pratt's Walk is about as close a match to the architecture of Blake's house as is to be found in the area.

Continue along Lambeth Road and turn left into Lambeth High Street just opposite St Mary's church (now the Garden Museum)

In such a ravaged townscape, clues can be found in the surviving street names. Walk past Norfolk Row and another Lambeth poet is conjured: Henry Howard, Earl of Surrey and son of the Duke of Norfolk, grew up in the ducal house on this site in the early sixteenth century. Catherine Howard was to be found here too, better remembered as one of King Henry's shorter-lived wives than as Surrey's first cousin. One of Howard's verses endures over the road in St Mary's Lambeth church. The epitaph he wrote to his esquire, Thomas Clere, was carved for that knight's tomb and was originally set in the floor to the north side of the chancel; now it is mounted on the wall.

Norfolk sprung thee; Lambeth holds thee dead...

Blake's apprentice work had been done among the tombs in Westminster Abbey, sketching the sculpted heads of Kings and Queens. In adult life, organised religion would probably never have brought him into St Mary's church, but did he linger here once over Howard's epitaph?

On the left along Lambeth High Street the entrance gates to Old Paradise Gardens with their etched metal designs taken from the illustrated pages of old herbals and with their fragments of text salvaged from tombstones are suggestive of the copper plates that Blake engraved and etched to create his illuminated books. 'Old Paradise' is a renaming borrowed from a neighbouring street; until recently this was the Old Lambeth Burial Ground – an eighteenth century overspill for the dead for whom there was no longer room in the overflowing churchyard of St Mary's. It closed for burials in 1852 and the decipherable words of its few remaining headstones have provided some of the texts on the gates.

Old Paradise Gardens: both the name and the space remind one of Blake's short lyric *The Garden of Love* which he wrote in Lambeth and included in the *Songs of Experience*. Although this former burial ground is not quite the pre-lapsarian state that Blake laments at the beginning of that poem, it is now at least returned to the condition of a garden. Within its green space flowering shrubs and trees have been allowed to re-assert themselves and the tombstones have been tidied away against walls or artfully grouped among brickwork. Children do play on the green and, always excepting the few park regulations imposed by Lambeth Council, 'Thou shalt not' has been taken down from over the door.

> *I went to the Garden of Love,*
> *And saw what I never had seen:*
> *A Chapel was built in the midst,*
> *Where I used to play on the green.*
>
> *And the gates of this Chapel were shut,*
> *And Thou shalt not. writ over the door;*

So I turn'd to the Garden of Love,
That so many sweet flowers bore.

And I saw it was filled with graves,
And tomb-stones where flowers should be:
And Priests in black gowns, were walking their rounds,
And binding with briars, my joys & desires.

Continue down Lambeth High Street past the Windmill PH. Turn right onto Black Prince Road to reach the Albert Embankment and the River Thames. Pause at the seats by White Hart Dock

I wander thro' each charter'd street
Near where the charter'd Thames does flow
And mark in every face I meet
Marks of weakness, marks of woe

In every cry of every Man,
In every Infants cry of fear,
In every voice: in every ban,
The mind-forg'd manacles I hear

The precise location of the 'charter'd streets' near to the Thames that Blake describes in the opening stanza of *London* can never really be known. Indeed the sense of disorientation that pervades the poem suggests that Blake did not wish to precisely locate it. And yet when Blake began composing *London* he had been living in Lambeth for three years and his new house was a short walk from both Westminster Bridge and from Lambeth stairs, the point on the river where Lambeth Bridge now is. He had of course lived far longer in Westminster, but at a much greater distance from the Thames. Blake could easily walk to the river at Lambeth Stairs by going down Hercules Buildings and turning right along Lambeth Road. It offers an attractive hypothetical location for the poem. Immediately to the south of the stairs and running along Fore

Street and Princes Street (now the Albert Embankment) was the original village of Water Lambeth. By the 1790s this had become an overcrowded and uneasy mix of industry and poor housing that was prone to flooding. Many of the buildings in its tight network of streets had been given over to potteries, boat builders and small workshops; its medieval houses had become beer shops and poor lodgings. If there were to be a local Lambeth inspiration for *London*'s 'charter'd' streets, then this could be the place that Blake had in mind. In his first draft of the poem he had written "each dirty street/Near where the dirty Thames does flow", a description which certainly described Water Lambeth. Blake's other access point to the Thames at Westminster Bridge and then along Bishops Walk in front of Lambeth Palace was a much more tidy and managed area.

It requires a double act of the imagination to relate the present street scene with those which Blake would have experienced. Lambeth's riverside here has been multiply transformed and is still transforming, in its most recent incarnation into an increasingly exclusive, gated domain of private and premium riverside views. The approach to White Hart Dock along Lambeth High Street and past the fragment of the Windmill PH is effected down a canyon of high and higher grand-standing buildings. South Bank House, built as Doulton's potteries office and show rooms on the corner of Black Prince Road, with its wedding cake display of faïence and tile work (for the would-be builders of Knightsbridge and Russell Square) has been shrunk to a mere bauble beside the skyline of an enlarging hotel. White Hart Dock, decked with clumsy public art, is the only other relic of this area's industrial past.

However, the late-Victorian version of Lambeth that can be reconstructed from these fragments would itself have been unknown to Blake. The potteries and factories that Blake would have encountered fronted directly onto the Thames. By 1870 they had all been taken down and rebuilt as part of the construction of the Albert Embankment. The old village of Lambeth was demolished in an area clearance as comprehensive as anything since imposed in the borough. In its stead, the Albert Embankment – a combination of sewer, flood protection and new highway – was laid across Lambeth's ruins and Doultons and all the other businesses that had lined the river were rebuilt on the land side of the Embankment. A series of draw docks, of which White Hart Dock is the sole survivor, were dug to maintain river access for these businesses: barges might still pass under the roadway to load and unload raw materials and finished goods.

Today the Albert Embankment with its elegant cast iron lamps, its wide paving, and with the Thames Path running alongside it with views across to the heart of Westminster, suggests that the Thames has always been an open river. This too is deeply misleading. Prior to1870 and certainly when Blake knew it, access to the Thames in London, apart from at its few public stairs and toll bridges, was closed off by the businesses that lined its banks. Perhaps this is why in *London* Blake uses the word *charter'd*, (an intriguing multi-facetted word that suggests power, ownership and control – and in stark contrast to the personal experiences and the 'weakness and woe' of the inhabitants of the same streets) to describe the river and why he is careful to describe the streets as 'near', rather than 'on', the Thames. For the river here, hemmed in by the private frontages of timber wharfs, potteries, bone boilers, whiting works and other manufactories, would not have been visible to him. We can turn to archive images, and particularly to those photographs taken just before the demolition of the area in the mid-1860s, to get a sense of these same dirty, claustrophobic and charter'd streets through which he could have wandered.

(OPPOSITE) Lambeth's 'charter'd streets' beside the Thames? Upper Fore Street just before demolition for the Albert Embankment, ca 1865

Cross over the Albert Embankment and turn right to walk north along the Thames path, pass under Lambeth Bridge, then take the path to the right at Lambeth Pier and cross back over Lambeth Palace Road to Lambeth Palace and pause at the seats in St Mary's Gardens

Standing before the red-brick battlements of Lambeth Palace's Morton Tower and the white rag-stone of Lambeth's former parish church, Lambeth's twin towers, once again it is lines from *London* which connect us with Blake's experience of this place. The voice of Blake's chimney sweep is already known to us. With that 'cry', Blake is referring us back to the opening lines of an earlier poem within *Experience, The Chimney Sweeper,*

> *A little black thing among the snow:*
> *Crying weep, weep, in notes of woe*

The young boys sent to climb up and sweep out chimneys would have cried 'Sweep', but in Blake's state of 'experience' in Lambeth, their cry has become contracted and he hears instead the word 'weep'. It isn't just the injustice enshrined in that grim cry which 'appalls' the blackened churches; nor is it just the actual 'pall' of soot dislodged by the sweeps' labour that has blackened their whited sepulchres. What equally angers Blake is the hypocrisy, power ('Thou shalt not') and wealth of the established church (already defined as 'binding with briars my joys and desires') which is blackening London. And he writes this from his house in Lambeth, overlooking the palace of the head of the English established church.

> *How the Chimney-sweepers cry*
> *Every blackning Church appalls,*
> *And the hapless Soldiers sigh*
> *Runs in blood down Palace walls*

Blake was not an 'educated' man in the current sense of that word. He was the apprenticed son of a Westminster hosier. But through his own efforts he became highly cultured and widely-read with a largely self-taught and radically inflected sense of history, influenced no doubt by the informal political circles in which he had moved. He knew Thomas Paine, the author of *The Rights of Man*, and in the early years of the French Revolution Blake had walked the streets of London and Lambeth wearing the red cap of Liberty. He would have linked key populist moments in English history such as the Peasants Revolt and the Laudian riots of 1640 (when Lambeth Palace was attacked and the Archbishop forced to flee) with his own personal experiences of more recent events. As a young man he had seen blood on the streets in 1780 when he was caught up in the anti-Catholic and anti-Government Gordon Riots. During these riots another Archbishop, Cornwallis, had been forced to flee Lambeth Palace in a small boat while a regiment of foot soldiers at the gates kept the mob at bay.

While he was working on the *Songs of Experience* in 1793 Blake was still a radical republican and still (just) a supporter of the French Revolution. On one level the blood on the palace walls refers to the Bastilles that were being stormed across Europe by France's citizen armies. But it is a capacious enough image to hold within it an allusion to that older strain of English radical history. So is the convergence here with Lambeth Palace mere coincidence or a trace memory? Do the palace walls and the heavy gates of the Morton's Tower, defended by troops against the mob in 1640 and again in 1780, also suggest the *soldier's sigh* that *runs in blood down Palace walls?*

Go out of St Mary's Gardens and re-join Lambeth Road. Follow the yellow brick wall east past the former parish school and turn left (north) down the small alley that leads into Archbishops Park

Hercules Road and the site of Blake's house lies just beyond the eastern edge of the park, across the railway line that we have already passed under and which closes off the view. Blake would have been able see the edge of the Palace's grounds from the top floor window of Hercules Buildings; the west side of the road was still fields and market gardens and beyond Carlisle Lane was the high brick wall of the archbishops' garden.

The open grassy spaces of Archbishops Park with their democratic planting, picnic tables, public tennis courts and outdoor gym equipment conceal the earlier and at times angry and contested history of what had been a very private space. The high wire fence to the left of the path separates the public park from the Archbisop's garden of Lambeth Palace – from which yet larger extent the park was carved out in 1900. Even after that reduction, the palace grounds beyond the wire are still the second-largest private garden in London after Buckingham Palace.

Go to the left to follow the path around the edge of the park to the North West corner and exit onto Lambeth Palace Road. Turn right and cross Royal Street

Crouching under the very walls of Lambeth Palace, where your grace has the pleasant responsibility of illustrating the opulence and paternal sympathy of the legal church of the land, lie streets as dismal, cheerless and discreditable as any that God in his wrath permitted to remain unconsumed. In the houses are polluted air, squalor, dirt and pale faced children. The only green thing upon which their feverish eyes could look is enclosed in your Grace's Palace park and shut out from their sight by dead walls... Go into these houses (as the writer of this memorial has) and see how a blank wall has been kept up so that no occupant of the rooms may look upon grass or tree, and the window which admits light and air has been turned, by the order of a former archbishop, the opposite way upon an outlook as wretched as the lot of the inhabitants.
- George Jacob Holyoake, 1878

The political campaign to shame the Archbishop into releasing some of his gardens to create a public open space had kicked off in the 1870s and was fronted by the secularist George Jacob Holyoake who, never mind his natural antipathy to the power and wealth of the established church, had become particularly incensed by the gross disparity between the Archbishop of Canterbury in his palace and his immediate neighbours in the back-to-back slum houses of Royal Street. The fact that the Archbishop was the ground landlord of this warren of mean streets only added an additional grim irony to his campaign. The specific detail that enraged Holyoake and which he used to deadly rhetorical effect was the fact that the back walls of the houses on Royal Street which abutted onto Lambeth Palace's garden had no windows. This had been stipulated in the building leases by a previous Archbishop who, while happy to accrue the ground rents from these slums, did not want the poor of Lambeth looking over his garden wall. So in 1878 Holyoake wrote a monumentally angry open letter to Archbishop Tait which he also had published in the *The Times*, noting the wicked contrast on either side of the wall: "the sheep in the Palace grounds were fat and florid and the children in the street were lean and pallid". Holyoake's public shaming of the archbishopric took a while to take effect. It would take another 22 years and another two incumbents before Archbishop Temple oversaw the transfer of this portion of his garden to become a public park.

> *Every house a den, every man bound; the shadows are fill'd With spectres, and the windows wove over with curses of iron: Over the doors Thou shalt not; & over the chimneys Fear is written: With bands of iron round their necks fasten'd into the walls The citizens: in leaden gyves the inhabitants of suburbs Walk heavy: soft and bent are the bones of villagers.* – Europe, 1794

In the 1790s Blake was able to look in on the grounds of the palace from the top floor of his house in Hercules Buildings. He would have been all too aware of the large private park that he had to negotiate the walled extent of to reach Lambeth riverside. While he despised organised religion and the established church, Blake was not a secularist either. Nor is it a complete anachronism to suggest that the idea of turning a private garden into a public park would have concerned Blake. One senses his position in poems like *The Garden of Love*, and of course one can mine his other writings to find evidence to suggest that morally he would have lined up with the egalitarianism of a Holyoake against the privilege of an Archbishop. The imaginary "windows wove over with curses of iron" in Europe are suggestive of the grim dwellings that would shortly be built along Royal Street. Blake had been friends with Thomas Paine before Paine had to flee arrest and escape to France, and it was Paine, almost sounding like Blake before the event, who had previously written "the palaces of kings are built upon the ruins of the bowers of paradise".

Today on Royal Street, the last of the system built public housing awaits near certain demolition and re-invention. Canterbury House with its peeling concrete shells and 10 storeys of balconies had provided unusually democratic views across the Archbishops' gardens. Built in the 1960s, it was a response to the public-health horrors of that earlier slum version of Royal Street and, in its way, an extension of the campaign by nineteenth century radicals like Holyoake to secure decent housing for the poor. Today, like the slums that it replaced, it too feels like a relic of an earlier mode of living.

We return to where we began. Between Royal Street and the foot of Westminster Bridge the triumvirate of Becket House (12 storeys), DLD College (18 storeys) and the Park Plaza Westminster Bridge (12 storeys) suggests the future for Royal Street and a new template for Lambeth. St Thomas' Hospital's proposals for the demolition of Canterbury House are in abeyance, but the ongoing erosion of public space and public housing appears unstoppable.

The anxieties of the Archbishops about their privacy are now reflected back through a Brobdingnagian mirror. The four Lambeth hotels of the Park Plaza group, all passed on this walk, tower over our shoulders and over the river towards Westminster. Are these Lambeth's *new-charter'd streets*? The objections to loss of office space, to saturation and to the impact of tall buildings have been overruled and former government buildings, charities and industrial spaces have been stripped out for "upper upscale" hotel rooms with "stunning river views" – and the illusion of being in Westminster.

The image Blake used for the poem *London* shows a bearded old man being led by the hand by a young child through city streets. Unlike most of the images he drew to accompany the other Songs of Innocence and of Experience, this one does not directly reference the subject matter of the poem. Unusually Blake reuses this curious image in his later long poem *Jerusalem* and this time he provides us with a context that reaches back to help explain the earlier lyric and forward, perhaps, to help parse a London and a Lambeth that we are confronted with today.

> *I see London, blind and age bent begging thro the streets*
> *Of Babylon, led by a child. His tears run down his beard.*

Cross over Royal Street and continue walking north to return back to the foot of Westminster Bridge

***

As the remains of Blake's 'lovely Lambeth' are being once more transformed and when no building, seemingly, is worth as much as the future realisable value that can be fledged and phoenixed from its cleared site, can one even consider the question which buildings do we preserve and why?

In the first half of the nineteenth century no one outside Blake's small circle of patrons and disciples really knew anything of his work as an artist and poet. It was the work of later writers – such as Henry Crabb Robinson, Charles Lamb, the Rossetti brothers and Swinburne (in anthologising his poems and in tracking down and writing about his works) which rescued him from anonymity. Alexander Gilchrist's 1863 biography, *Life of William Blake*, "*Pictor Ignotus*", completed the process.

By the late-nineteenth century that process of recovery and discovery was well advanced. The collection of his art that is now held by Tate Britain was being built up by the British Museum; W B Yeats published an edition of his poetry in 1893; Lawrence Binyon published a book of his woodcuts in 1903. The auction sales of the Crewe collection and the Hodgson collection in 1903 and 1904, an exhibition of his art at the Carfax Gallery also in 1904 and the sale of the Linnell Collection (one of his original patrons and buyers) in 1918 released onto the market and into public consciousness many of his previously unseen works. Following on from this interest his various London homes also began to be revalued and a plaque was put on the outside of the modest terraced house that had now become no. 23 Hercules Road. The William Blake Society, formed in 1912 to nurture his reputation, wrote to *The Times* in that year to canvas interest in a memorial museum in one of his former houses. The society favoured one of the surviving Westminster houses either on South Molton Street or Broad Street. As for Hercules Road, it felt, "there would be serious difficulties in the way". Perhaps this was recognition of the house's poor state (elsewhere described as "in a damaged and derelict condition and palpably tottering to its end") but perhaps too it reflected the Blake Society's innate metropolitan prejudice: because it was located south of the river, this house was therefore less attractive.

It was the Corporation of London, the owner of the Hercules Road freeholds, who in seeking to construct "Homes for Heroes" after the First World War, closed off that awkward possibility. In November 1918 the Daily Mirror reported that "London was to lose the historic house in which the poet-painter William Blake lived for a number of years". Perhaps it was the combination of Armistice Day, a national influenza epidemic and the opening of the General Election campaign in the same week that meant that most other papers ignored the story. For most people, Lambeth was but a sea of unloved anonymous streets, either glimpsed at from across the river or looked down on from a railway carriage heading out of Waterloo. Protest was at best muted, the scheme was confirmed by mid-1919 and the houses were demolished. The four new blocks, each containing 48 flats, were under construction in 1923 and complete by 1926, at which point the old blue plaque, still with the wrong dates, was re-erected on the front wall of Blake House at the point where 13 Hercules Buildings had once stood.

Floor plan of one the flats of Blake House, 1919

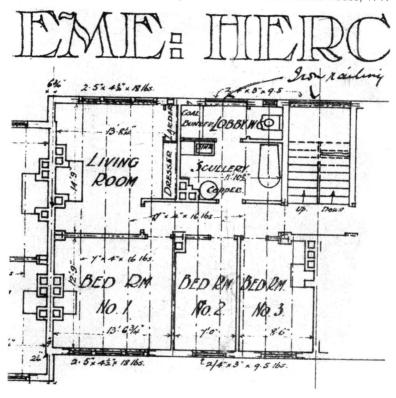

Hindsight is a useful device. Blake's house – which the Corporation, and to an extent the Blake Society, had consigned for demolition as one more dried-up pea in the ramshackle pod of a South London streetscape – would be seen differently today had it survived. But back in 1918, Number 23 Hercules Road was an embarrassment ripe for slum-clearance, even though a century and a quarter earlier it had been the happiest of all Blake's London homes. Back then it had still looked across fields and it had both a front and a back garden with an "Arcadian arbour... in the shadow of a grape vine". Blake said he never enjoyed any of his etching-painting rooms so much as "the panelled back room looking on the garden in Lambeth". Here he would work facing the light at his long engravers table beneath the window that gave onto the poplar trees and Astley's house at the bottom of the garden. It was the house in which he was his most imaginatively productive, often working through the night to capture his visions on the page, sometimes waking Catherine to sit with him. It was certainly the place where he was his most physically productive; he had "a whole house to range in", one which was large enough to accommodate his rolling press from which he would pull the prints that were assembled into his books of songs, poems and prophecy – all of which bore on their title page (prosaically, playfully, proudly?) that colophon, *Lambeth, Printed by W. Blake.*

Blake left Hercules Buildings in 1800. An opportunity had arisen for him to live and work in Sussex, which he did for three years before returning to Westminster (where he would remain until his death in 1827, his last residence was a two-room apartment in Fountain Court just off The Strand). He left his home on a summer's day of the new century loaded with the productions of his Lambeth decade; the chaise that was taking him to Felpham laboured up and over Brixton Hill, burdened with "sixteen heavy boxes and portfolios full of prints". He would never return to South London, yet after he had abandoned it, another 'Lambeth' started to emerge in his writings, not a tangible place that could be found on a map or walked through as he once had. Instead a highly personal Lambeth of the imagination began to emerge, which lived on for Blake, the mental traveller, and continued to resound mysteriously through the poetry of his final books, *Milton* and *Jerusalem.*

There is a grain of sand in Lambeth that Satan cannot find
Nor can his watch fiends find it; 'tis translucent and has many angles.
But he who finds it will find Oothoon's palace, for within,
opening into Beulah, every angle is a lovely heaven.

—⚏—

Acknowledgements
Cover design and map taken from Horwood's map of London, 1807.
Illustrations credits:
  pp. 5, 10, 13, 14, 23, 31   Lambeth Archives

Thanks to Michael Phillips for reading and commenting on the text, to the staff at Lambeth Archives for their help and to all the Crowdfunder supporters and Arts Council England for their financial assistance.

GOING FURTHER

If this walk booklet has left you wanting to find out more about William Blake then there are a number of ways in to his work. All of his books are now available as colour facsimiles and it is these, rather than just the extracted text of his poetry, that are the better way to appreciate his particular genius. *Songs of Innocence and of Experience* remains the best known, most accessible and most rewarding of the illuminated books; *Milton* and *Jerusalem* are a delight for the initiated. The difficulty with reading others about Blake is in knowing where to start; like the 'grain of sand in Lambeth', there are 'many angles' and many agendas. Mona Wilson and Peter Ackroyd have both produced interpretative biographies in the twentieth century but arguably Alexander Gilchrist's *Life* of 1863, which is still in print, is still the closest to a definitive account of Blake's life. The best collections of his work as an artist are in Tate Britain, London and the Fitzwilliam Museum in Cambridge.